WATER

experimenting with science

Antonella Meiani

Lerner Publications Company • Minneapolis

First American edition published in 2003 by Lerner Publications Company

Published by arrangement with Istituto Geografico DeAgostini, Novara, Italy

Originally published as *Il Grande Libro degli Esperimenti*

Copyright © 1999 by Istituto Geografico DeAgostini, Novara, Italy

Translated from the Italian by Maureen Spurgeon.
Translation copyright © 2000 by Brown Watson, England.

This book has been adapted from a single-volume work entitled *Il Grande Libro degli Esperimenti*, originally published by Istituto Geografico DeAgostini, Novara, Italy, in 1999. New back matter was developed by Lerner Publications Company.

Lerner Publications Company
A division of Lerner Publishing Group
241 First Avenue North
Minneapolis, MN 55401 U.S.A.

Website address: www.lernerbooks.com

Library of Congress Cataloging-in-Publication Data

Meiani, Antonella.
    [Il Grande libro degli esperimenti. English. Selections]
    Water / by Antonella Meiani ; [translated from the Italian by Maureen Spurgeon]
    1st American ed.
        p.   cm. — (Experimenting with science)
    Includes bibliographical references and index.
    Contents: 1. The surface tension of water—2. To float or not to float?—3. The transformation of water—4. Water solutions.—5. The force of water—Fact finder—Metric conversion chart.
    ISBN: 0–8225–0083–3 (lib. bdg. : alk. paper)
    1. Water—Experiments—Juvenile literature. [1. Water—Experiments. 2. Experiments.]
    I. Title.
QC145.24.M45132   2003
532—dc21   2001050773

Manufactured in the United States of America
1 2 3 4 5 6 – JR – 08 07 06 05 04 03

Table of Contents

The force of water 6

The surface tension of water....................12

To float or not to float? 18

The transformation of water....................24

Water solutions......................................30

Fact-Finder 34

Metric Conversion Table 35

Glossary 36

For Further Reading/Websites 37

Index 38

Water

How does water move? Why are drops of water round? Why do some things float and not others? Why does it rain? What happens to a substance when it dissolves in water? Find the answers to these and many more questions by doing the experiments in the following pages, under these headings:

- The force of water
- The surface tension of water
- To float or not to float?
- The transformation of water
- Water solutions

The force of water

Water, like all liquids, has no shape. It can occupy any space that is available.

It can flow downward, drawn by the force of gravity. When water falls, the force is so strong that this power can be converted into electrical energy. Yet, delicately and slowly, water can also rise up through the stem of a plant, keeping it alive.

The following experiments demonstrate many other features of water — the way it can seep through substances, its pressure, and the way it moves when it becomes warm.

How can water move?

WATER RISING UP

You need:
- stalk of celery, with leaves, about 20 cm (8 in.) long
- glass jar
- water
- blue or red food coloring

What to do:

1 Put water in the jar. Color the water with a few drops of food coloring.

2 Put the celery in the colored water. Then put the jar somewhere warm.

What happens?
After a few hours the stalk of celery and its leaves take on the same color as the water.

Why?
If you cut the celery, you will see that its ribs are like little tubes. The water has risen up through these narrow tubes and into the leaves. This is called capillary action. This is how plants absorb water from the ground through their roots, with the water rising up until it reaches the ends of their leaves. White flowers can sometimes be colored in the same way.

FLOWERS THAT FLOAT ON WATER

You need:
- sheet of paper
- colored pencils
- scissors
- soup plate with some water in it

What to do:

1 Draw the shape shown in the picture below. Color it in, then cut it out.

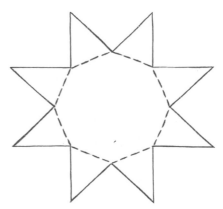

2 Fold the "petals" inwards along the dotted lines, as shown below.

3 Very carefully place the paper flower on the water.

What happens?
Slowly, the flower opens.

Why?
The water penetrates by capillary action into the little empty spaces between the fibers of the paper. This makes the fibers swell, including those along the folds. This swelling makes the petals unfold, and so the flower opens out.

Water can move downward, but it can also rise up
by means of capillary action.

Can you increase the force of water?

THE WEIGHT OF WATER

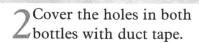

You need:

- two plastic bottles
- one nail
- duct tape
- water

What to do:

1 Using the nail, poke a vertical line of holes in one bottle. Poke a horizontal line of holes in the other bottle, as shown in the picture. (Do this with the help of an adult.)

2 Cover the holes in both bottles with duct tape.

3 Fill the bottles with water. Remove the tape from one bottle, then from the other.

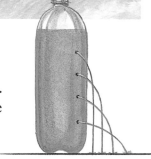

What happens?

Water spurts out at an equal distance all around the bottle with holes in a horizontal line. But water spurts out at different distances from the bottle with the holes in a vertical line. The lower the hole, the farther the water goes.

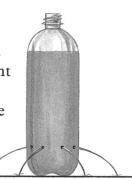

Why?

The water presses heavily against the inside of the bottles, and so it escapes through the holes with considerable force. This force is strongest where a lot of water pushes against the inside of the bottle (where the water is deepest) and so the water spurts farther.

Deep-sea exploration

A bathyscaphe is a submersible (underwater vessel) that is used for exploration and research at great depths of the oceans. The hull of the bathyscaphe houses the engine and the tanks. As the bathyscaphe dives, these tanks are gradually filled with water to balance the internal pressure with the external pressure of the water. Beneath the hull is a sphere of steel, strong enough to withstand the pressure of the water at great depths. This sphere is for the crew and their observation instruments. In 1960, Jacques Piccard (son of Auguste Piccard, who invented the bathyscaphe) and Lt. Don Walsh of the U.S. Navy went 11,022 meters (35,800 ft.) in the bathyscaphe *Trieste III* to the floor of the Pacific Ocean, as deep as it is possible to go.

A SIMPLE FOUNTAIN

You need:
- plastic tube
- tape
- the glass (or plastic) tube part of an eyedropper
- funnel
- water

What to do:

1 Tape the funnel to one end of the plastic tube and the eyedropper to the other.

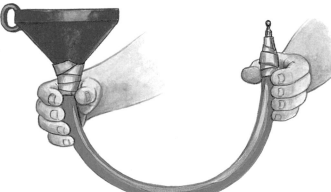

2 Working over a sink, close the opening of the dropper with your finger and fill the tube with water through the funnel.

3 Lower the end with the dropper and take away your finger.

What happens?
A spurt of water escapes from the dropper. The higher the funnel, the higher the water spurts.

Why?
The pressure exerted by the air on the opening of the funnel is greater than the pressure of the water inside the tube, so the water is pushed upward. Raising the funnel makes the water spurt higher, because the water in the tube is falling from a greater height. Raising an object farther above Earth's surface makes the object fall with greater force.

The natural force of water

The energy of water has been used for centuries to drive waterwheels. This energy may be from falling water or water flowing below the waterwheel. The power from the force of water flowing down from mountains is used by hydroelectric plants to produce electrical power.

Water has more force when it is subjected to the pressure of the air above it.

Why does heat make water move about?

WATER AND HEAT

You need:
- see-through bowl or basin
- small glass jar with a lid
- food coloring
- water

What to do:

1 Fill the bowl or basin with cold water.

2 Put a few drops of food coloring in the jar and ask an adult to fill it with hot (not boiling) water. Then put the lid on the jar.

3 Put the jar in the bowl or basin, making sure that the cold water completely covers it. Remove the lid.

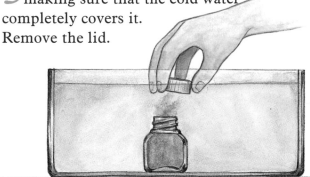

What happens?
The colored water escapes from the jar and rises up, spreading out along the surface. After a few moments it begins to descend and to mix with the rest of the water.

Why?
Like all matter, water is made up of tiny, moving particles called molecules. Heat speeds up the movement of the molecules, and they move away from each other. As they spread out, they become less dense (less tightly packed together) and so the water becomes lighter. That is why the colored hot water "floats" on the cold water. As the heat spreads and the colored water cools, it descends and begins to mix with the rest of the water.

How water heats up in a saucepan

Saucepans are generally made of aluminum or steel. Aluminum and steel are good conductors of heat, both containing and transmitting heat. So the saucepan heats up on contact with heat and heats up the water at the bottom. The heated water rises up. Colder water takes its place, then this too gets hot and rises up. These movements of rising and falling allow the heat to spread through all the water in the saucepan. We call these movements *convection*. Heat moves around in the air in the same way.

Why do underwater divers use wet suits?

Water, like air, is a poor conductor of heat. It cannot contain heat, nor can it give off heat. A diver's wet suit creates a thin layer of water that prevents cold water from coming in contact with the skin, so that the body's heat is not lost. Also, the wet suit is made with insulating material. This material keeps heat in.

Sea currents

Sailors travel continually through warm and cold currents. These are streams that run through seawater and affect the state of the oceans and the rest of Earth. Currents are generated by winds and differences in temperature and salt content. Currents of cold water (which is denser and heavier) that come from the seas at the North and South Poles flow at the lowest depths of the oceans. Currents of warm water (lighter and less dense) come from tropical and equatorial seas and flow closer to the surface of the oceans. The currents mix the seawater, carrying oxygen to the deepest regions and distributing minerals to the living things under the sea. They also affect the climate and change the temperature along the coasts they pass near. For example, the warm Gulf Current comes from the Caribbean Sea and moves towards Europe, where it warms the climate of the oceanic coasts. The cold current from Labrador in northern Canada cools the Atlantic coasts of the United States, bringing very harsh winters.

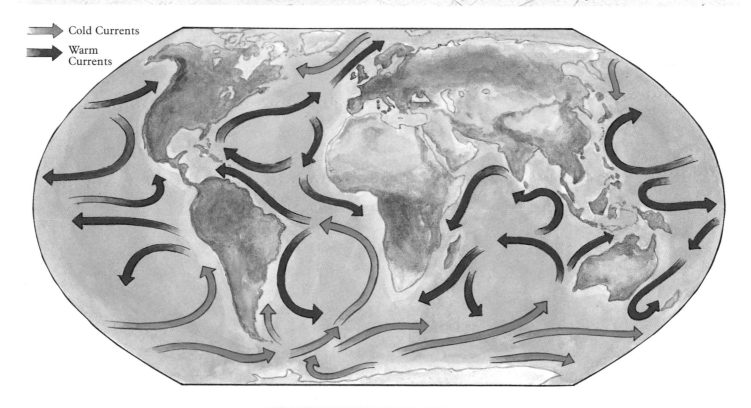

Cold Currents

Warm Currents

Warm water is lighter than cold water, so warm water rises above cold water.

The surface tension of water

Water is fluid; it can be poured and you can make things sink into it. Its molecules move, but they do not separate completely because they are constantly attracted to each other. The molecules on the surface of the water do not have other molecules to attract them from above, so they bind together more strongly. It is this surface tension that makes it possible for some creatures to walk on water — and for us to make soap bubbles.

Why are drops of water round?

SUSPENDED ON WATER

You need:
- tweezers
- needle
- a glass
- water

What to do:

1 Fill the glass with water up to the brim.

2 Pick up the needle with the tweezers and very gently place it on the surface of the water.

What happens?
The needle floats. (You may find that the needle sinks to the bottom. Try again. It is very important to place it slowly and horizontally.)

Why?
The molecules of water on the surface form a sort of film that can support a light object. This force that holds the molecules together is called surface tension. When you fill the glass to the brim, look closely at the surface of the water. The water curves slightly above the brim. This curve is caused by surface tension, which pulls tightly to contain the water like a bag. If there is only a little water, the surface tension will make it form into a round drop.

A BARRIER OF MATERIAL

You need:
- handkerchief
- rubber band
- a glass
- water

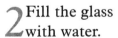

What to do:

1 Put the hand-kerchief in water. Then wring it out.

2 Fill the glass with water.

3 Stretch the handkerchief tightly over the glass. Hold it in place with the rubber band.

4 Working over a sink, quickly turn the glass upside down.

What happens?
The water stays in the glass, as if the handkerchief were waterproof.

Why?
When you dampened the handkerchief, the water filled up the little spaces between the fibers of the material. The surface tension creates a tight barrier through which the water cannot penetrate. Wet hairs clinging together in locks and damp sand that can be modeled without cracking are other examples of water holding fibers and particles together by filling up the spaces in between.

Walking on water

The water strider and water treader are small pond-dwelling insects. They can run or slide on the surface of the water in search of their prey without sinking. Under their feet, the "skin" of the surface tension of the water bends inward, but it is strong enough to support the insects without breaking.

Surface tension creates a membrane that can contain a small quantity of water in a little, round drop.

How does soap act in water?

HOLES IN WATER

You need:
- talcum powder
- water
- liquid soap
- sink or bowl

What to do:

1 Fill the sink or bowl with water.

2 Sprinkle talcum powder on the surface of the water.

3 Dip your finger into the water here and there, as if you were poking holes in it.

What happens?
The talcum powder helps you see the surface tension of the water. Your finger pierces the surface tension, but the "hole" closes up again.

Why?
The surface tension is a strong force. It is broken only momentarily when you poke it with your finger.

4 Now put a drop of liquid soap on your finger. (Be careful to do this away from the sink to avoid getting soap in the water.) Then put the soapy finger into the water, close to the edge of the sink.

5 Poke holes in the talcum-powdered water with the soapy finger.

What happens?
The first time you dip your soapy finger in the water, the talcum powder moves away. But the next time you dip it into the talcum-powder surface, your finger leaves "holes."

Why?
The soap loosens the tension at the place where you dip your finger. The tension is stronger on the rest of the surface, so it attracts and holds back the talcum powder. The holes left by the soapy finger do not close again, because in these places the soap prevents the water molecules from joining together again. So the surface "skin" cannot regain its unbroken state. If you want to repeat the experiment, you will need to change the water.

A SOAP BOAT

You need:
- basin or sink
- piece of cardboard
- scissors
- liquid soap
- water

What to do:

1 Fill the basin or sink with water.

2 Cut a triangle shape from the cardboard. When the water is still, float the cardboard triangle in a corner of the basin or sink, pointing toward the center.

3 Put a little soap on the tip of one finger. (Do this away from the sink.) Then put the soapy finger in the water behind your cardboard "boat."

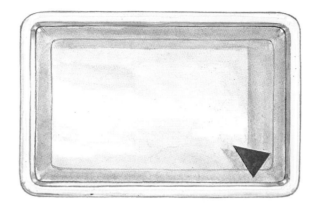

What happens?
The boat shoots forward toward the opposite side of the basin or sink.

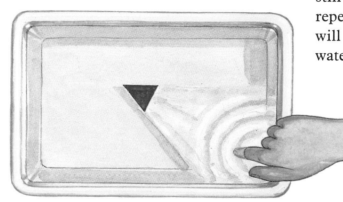

Why?
At the beginning of the experiment, the boat stayed still because the surface tension was pulling it in all directions. The soap lessens the tension behind the boat. This means that the boat is pulled forward into the area where the surface tension is still strong. If you want to repeat the experiment, you will have to change the water.

How soap works

Water alone is not able to remove the dirt from clothes, plates, or skin, especially if the dirt is greasy. There are two main types of molecules in detergents – those that attract and cling to the small particles of dirt and those that dissolve in the water, keeping the water molecules from coming together. The detergent breaks up the dirt and removes it from the object being washed. Then it spreads the dirt out into the water, ready to be drained away.

Soap weakens the force that keeps water molecules together.

How are soap bubbles made?

CONCENTRIC DOMES

You need:
- soap bubble liquid (put this in the refrigerator for about an hour)
- drinking straw
- smooth surface to work on (something like glass, plastic, or steel)

What to do:

1 Moisten the work surface.

2 Dip the straw into the soap. Blow a bubble and slowly place it on the surface. The bubble will become a dome.

3 Dip the straw deep into the soap, making sure the straw gets wet. Insert the straw very carefully into the first dome and blow gently to form a second dome.

4 Make a third dome in the same way. (Work very carefully, so that each new dome does not touch the ones that you made before.)

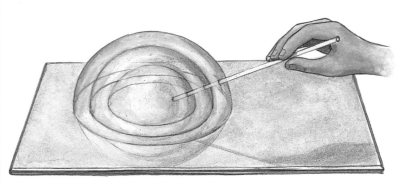

What happens?

Each bubble positions itself at the center of the domes you made before, and it makes the others grow bigger.

Why?

There is air inside the bubbles. Each new bubble pushes against the air inside the one before, and the outside bubbles grow larger because their soapy surface is elastic. The more you try this experiment, the more different structures you will find you can create by placing the bubbles on the surface and seeing how much your bubble mix can expand.

Recipes for soap bubbles

To make lasting bubbles, try these recipes. Which one is the best?

○ 600g (2½ c.) water + 200g (¾ c.) liquid dish detergent + 100g (⅓ c.) glycerine

○ 600g (2½ c.) hot distilled water + 300g (1 c.) glycerine + 50g (½ c.) detergent powder + 50g (10 tsp.) ammonia. The liquid must rest for a few days, then it needs to be filtered and kept in a refrigerator for 12 hours before use.

○ 300g (1¼ c.) water + 300g (1¼ c.) liquid dish detergent + 2 teaspoons sugar

○ 5 tablespoons grated hand soap in 400g (1¾ c.) hot water (it works even better to dissolve the soap in water over a source of heat). Store the liquid for a week, then add two teaspoons of sugar.

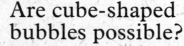

BOUNCING BUBBLES

You need:
- something made of wool (a sweater or scarf)
- soap bubble liquid (chill this in the refrigerator for about an hour)
- table tennis paddle (you can also use a little tray or a hardcover book)

What to do:

1 Wrap the wool item around the paddle.

2 Blow a bubble, so that it lands on the wool.

3 Gently move the paddle to bounce the bubble.

What happens?
The bubble lies on the wool without changing shape or breaking, and it bounces!

Why?
The surface of the bubble is made up of water and soap and this is flexible (bendable) enough to land on the wool and stay, remaining suspended on it without breaking. If you want to play this game on a cold day, try taking your wool-covered paddle and bubble outside. The bubble will freeze and look like a crystal.

Are cube-shaped bubbles possible?

The tension "skin" that soap makes will stretch as far as it can. But this skin always wants to close up into a shape where the volume of air inside it is as small as possible – a sphere. So bubbles of other shapes cannot be blown naturally. But more unusual bubbles can be created using a piece of wire. If the soap solution is flexible enough, it may be possible to make soap-bubble cubes or pyramids.

Soap reduces the surface tension of water, thus allowing the air inside a bubble to expand.

To float or not to float?

Swimmers know the feeling of weightlessness when they move or float in the water. But weightlessness is not just a sensation, it is a reality. Water supports solid objects, canceling out some of their weight.

The following experiments show what is needed for an object to float, and how some very heavy objects such as ocean liners stay afloat.

Why do things seem to weigh less in water?

WHAT THE DYNAMOMETER REVEALS

You need:
- dynamometer (an instrument for measuring force)
- apple
- thin string
- deep bowl
- water
- pen and paper

What to do:

1 Tie one end of the string to the stalk of the apple and the other end to the dynamometer. Write down how much force the dynamometer measures.

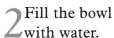

2 Fill the bowl with water.

3 Immerse the apple in water without taking it off the dynamometer. Write down how much force the dynamometer measures now.

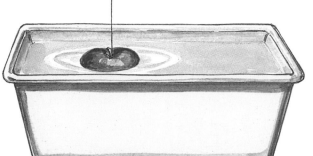

What happens?
When the apple is in the water, the dynamometer measures less force.

Why?
When the apple is immersed, it moves a certain amount of water. The water it moves tries to take up its position again, and presses against the apple, pushing it up towards the top. This push is called displacement and is the same as the weight of the water that the apple has moved. So if an object weighing 500g (18 oz.) is immersed and moves 200g (7 oz.) of water, it gets an upward push that reduces its weight by 200g (7 oz.). Therefore, when immersed, that object will show a weight of 300g (11 oz.).

Archimedes' Principle

Have you noticed that when you get into the bathtub, the level of the water rises? This simple fact is said to have been the inspiration for the Greek scientist Archimedes, who lived in Syracuse, Greece, in the third century A.D. After noting the rising of his bathwater, he carried out many experiments, not only with water but also with other liquids, to prove his theory of the displacement of water and establish Archimedes' Principle. This rule states that an object immersed in liquid is given an upward thrust that is equal to the weight of the liquid that the object has moved.

An object in water is given an upward thrust that is equal to the weight of the water displaced by the object.

Why do some things float and not others?

A QUESTION OF SHAPE

You need:
- modeling clay
- saucepan lid
- bowl
- water

What to do:

1 Fill the bowl with water.

2 Mold the modeling clay into a boat shape and place it on the water.

3 Now roll the boat-shaped clay into a ball. Place this on the water.

What happens?
The little boat floats on top. The ball sinks to the bottom.

4 Now place the saucepan lid on the water, first horizontally, then vertically.

What happens?
When it is horizontal, the saucepan lid floats. When it is vertical, it sinks to the bottom.

Why?
The more water that is displaced by an object, the greater the upward thrust that the object gets. With the clay boat and the horizontal saucepan lid, a wide surface floats on the water, and therefore they each displace a lot of water. So they each get an upward thrust that is sufficient to keep them afloat. The clay ball and the vertical saucepan lid displace less water, so the upward thrust that they get is not enough to keep them afloat. This experiment shows that floating depends on the shape of an object, not just its weight.

LIMIT OF FLOATING

You need:
- modeling clay
- small objects, such as paper clips, marbles, dice, pebbles
- basin
- water

What to do:
1 Mold the modeling clay into a little tub, as you see in the picture.

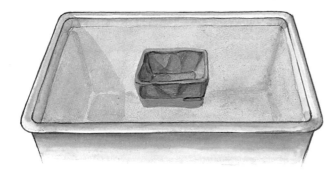

2 Fill the basin with water and float the clay tub on the water. Make a notch on the tub to mark the level of the water.

3 One at a time, put the small objects in the tub and see if the notch goes below the level of the water.

What happens?
The more objects you place in the tub, the lower it sinks into the water.

Why?
The tub is concave, which means it bends inward, and it contains air. When it is filled with objects the tub weighs more, but keeps its same size, which means it has a greater density. (Density means the weight contained within a volume of space.) As long as the displaced water weighs more than the tub and its contents, the tub stays afloat. When the weight of the tub is more than that of the water that it has displaced, the tub will sink. This experiment shows that the ability to float also depends on the density of the object that is put into the water.

Ships and submarines
Even when they are built from very dense materials, such as steel, ships do not sink because inside they have hollow areas full of air. Their density is therefore less than that of the water. Submarines are able to float and to dive whenever they need, by altering their density. A submarine has tanks that can be filled with water to make the submarine dive, then emptied when it needs to rise up to the surface again.

Which is denser, wood or iron?
A wooden marble will float when it is put in water; but an iron ball of the same size (and displacing the same amount of water) sinks to the bottom. This is because iron is denser than both wood and water. If an object is denser than water, it will sink, because it cannot displace its weight in water.

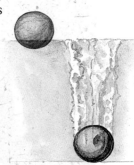

Whether an object floats or not depends on its shape and its density.

Do gases and liquids float in water?

JUMPING MOTHBALLS

You need:
- mothballs
- vinegar
- baking soda
- water
- glass jar
- spoon

What to do:

1 Fill the jar with water, then add two spoons of vinegar and two of baking soda. Mix thoroughly.

2 Put the mothballs in the water. (If they feel very smooth, scratch them a little to make them rough.)

What happens?
At first, the mothballs go to the bottom. But after a short time, little bubbles attach themselves to the surface of the balls and they begin to rise, then descend, then rise again.

Why?
The vinegar and baking soda, mixed together, produce a gas called carbon dioxide. This gas is released into the water in the form of little bubbles. Like all gases, carbon dioxide is lighter than water and so it rises. When the carbon dioxide attaches itself to the mothballs, it takes them with it as it rises to the top, where it disperses into the air. At this point, the mothballs become heavy again and sink to the bottom, then rise up, carried along by other bubbles of carbon dioxide.

TEST OF DENSITY

You need:
- see-through container
- liquid honey
- linseed or corn oil
- water

What to do:

1 Slowly pour some honey and then some oil into the jar.

2 Slowly pour in some water.

What happens?
The liquids do not mix, but separate into layers. The oil floats on the honey; the water sinks underneath the oil, but floats on the honey.

Why?
The three liquids have different densities. The oil, which has the lowest density, floats on the water. But the honey settles on the bottom because it has the greatest density.

THE EFFECT OF BRINE

You need:
- table salt
- large glass
- egg
- tablespoon
- large spoon
- water

What to do:

1 Fill the glass halfway with water. Then, using the spoon, carefully put the egg in the water.

What happens?
The egg sinks to the bottom of the glass.

2 Take the egg out of the water. Add 10 tablespoons of table salt, and mix until it is dissolved. Now you have made brine.

3 Put the egg in the water once more.

What happens?
The egg floats.

4 Take the egg out of the water again. Slowly add water to the glass until it is almost full.

5 Put the egg in the water again.

What happens?
The egg remains suspended in the center of the glass.

Why?
The egg is more dense than the water, and so it sinks. The saltwater (brine) is more dense than pure water, and therefore the egg floats. In the last stage of the experiment, the pure water floats on the brine because pure water has a lower density. The egg stays in the middle, because it is more dense than the pure water but less dense than the brine.

A sea of oil

Oil spills cause damage to the environment that is often impossible to clean up. Crude oil is so light that it floats on the sea. When it reaches the coast, crude oil covers the beaches and rocks and is impossible to remove. There are substances that can be sprayed on crude oil before it reaches coasts. They force the oil to the bottom of the sea. The oil still causes pollution, but the damage is less extensive than it would be on the surface.

There are some toys that use liquids of different densities. Because it is impossible for the two liquids shown here to mix, a fascinating wave effect is produced. In this toy, the boats have a density that is less than the blue liquid, but more than the clear liquid. This is why they stay suspended in the center.

All substances that have a lower density than water will float on it.

The transformation of water

Although water is a liquid, extreme cold will change it into a solid (such as ice, snow, or frost). Heat will change it into a gas that escapes into the air (water vapor). The following pages reveal the fascinating water cycle, with experiments that demonstrate how water forms into clouds, rain, or mist. Discover what happens when water is in the air, and why windows steam up in the winter.

How does heat dry something that is damp?

DISAPPEARING WATER

You need:
- two identical glasses
- small plate
- felt-tipped pen
- water

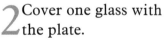

What to do:

1 Fill the two glasses with water to the same level. Mark this level with the felt-tipped pen.

2 Cover one glass with the plate.

3 Put the two glasses near a radiator, or in direct sunlight.

What happens?
The day after, the level of water in the uncovered glass is lower. The level in the covered jar is almost the same.

Why?
Because of the heat, the water in the uncovered glass has evaporated – transformed into tiny, invisible drops of water vapor that become absorbed into the air. This is how clothes that are hung up or spread out in the sun become dry. Moving air (such as the wind or our breath) also makes water evaporate. It moves the water vapor that comes off wet objects and makes it possible for the the air to absorb more water vapor.

Boiling point
When water reaches 100°C (212°F), it begins to boil. Bubbles of steam form in the liquid and escape into the air through the surface. The temperature of boiling changes with changes in air pressure. In high mountains, for example, the mass of air that hangs over Earth's surface is thinner, and so the atmospheric pressure is lower; therefore, water reaches the boiling point at a temperature of less than 100°C.

The energy of steam

Steam takes up more space than water (1,700 times as much!). Kept under pressure, steam produces enormous amounts of energy that can be used to power machines.

The first steam engine was invented in the second half of the eighteenth century. Steam was used to power machines in factories and locomotives that pulled trains. A century later, the steam engine was largely replaced by the internal combustion (gasoline) engine.

Geysers

Geysers are jets of steam that come from the interior of our planet. They erupt through cracks in Earth's surface and can reach a height of 10 meters (30 ft.). Their energy is called geothermal energy. It can be used to produce heat and electricity. There are many geysers throughout Iceland and in New Zealand and the United States.

The first steam locomotive was built in Great Britain at the beginning of the nineteenth century.

Heat makes water evaporate and disperse through the air.

Why does it rain?

RETURN TO THE LIQUID STATE

You need:
- saucepan
- metal lid
- hot plate
- water

What to do:

1 Fill the saucepan with water. Ask an adult to put it on the hot plate.

2 When the water boils, hold the lid up high in the cloud of steam that rises up from the water. Be careful to keep your hand away from the steam!

What happens?
Drops of water form under the lid.

Why?
Vapor rises up from the water as it boils and comes into contact with the cold lid. As this happens, the vapor loses heat and immediately returns to the liquid state. This phenomenon is called condensation.

Rain

With the heat of the Sun, water evaporates from lakes, rivers, seas, plants, and our skin. The enormous quantity of water vapor that rises up into the atmosphere cools and condenses into tiny drops of water that group together to form clouds. If a cloud encounters hot air, it disperses. If it encounters cold air, the drops of water join together into larger drops. They become too heavy to stay up in the air and fall to the ground in the form of rain.

WATER FROM NOTHING

You need:
- a glass
- freezer

What to do:

1 Make sure the glass is perfectly dry. Put it in the freezer.

2 After 30 minutes, take the glass out.

What happens?
Immediately, the glass steams up; soon after, tiny droplets of water form on the glass. If you touch it, your finger becomes damp.

Why?
In the freezer, the glass becomes very cold. When the glass is brought into contact with warm air, the glass cools the air next to it, and the water vapor in the air changes into tiny drops of water that mist up the glass. In winter, the windows of cars steam up because our breath, rich in water vapor, condenses into drops of water as soon as it comes into contact with the cold windows.

Humidity in the air

In the hottest days of the summer, when we feel hot and sticky, you will hear weather forecasters say that the humidity of the air is high. This means that there is a large quantity of water vapor in the air. When there is not much water vapor, the air is dry and our perspiration quickly evaporates. But when the humidity is high, there is already so much vapor in the air that our perspiration cannot evaporate.

Mist is made up of tiny drops of water that come from the condensation of water vapor in the atmospheric layers nearest the ground.

Cold air can hold only a little water vapor. If the night gets cool and the air is very humid, the water vapor condenses into tiny drops of dew that can be seen on leaves and on the ground in the morning.

When water vapor comes in contact with cold air, it condenses and becomes liquid water again. This is what causes rain.

Why do water pipes sometimes burst in the winter?

SOLID WATER

You need:
- glass or plastic jar with lid
- water
- freezer

What to do:

1 Fill the jar to the brim with water.

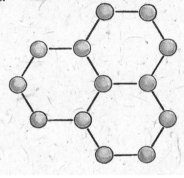

2 Place the lid on top of the jar, without screwing it down.

3 Carefully put the jar in the freezer and wait until the water in the jar has frozen.

What happens?
The water becomes solid. It rises above the rim of the jar, raising the lid.

Why?
When the water becomes ice, it takes up more space than when it is liquid, and so the jar cannot hold it all. If we were to leave a firmly-closed glass jar of water in the freezer, it would probably break because of the pressure of the ice. The pipes that carry drinking water and water for central heating in a house must be protected in winter and insulated from the cold so that they do not burst because of ice forming inside them.

The structure of molecules

Almost all substances spread out when they become warm. When they become cold again, they contract, or come closer together. Water contracts if the temperature drops, but if it becomes colder than 4°C (39°F), it begins to expand once again. This is due to the fact that below 4°C the molecules arrange themselves in a hexagonal pattern that takes up more space.

WHEN ICE MELTS

You need:
- a glass
- hot water
- ice cubes

What to do:

1 Fill the glass almost to the brim with hot water.

2 Put one or two ice cubes in the water. Ask some friends if they think the water will overflow when the cubes have melted.

What happens?
The level of the water stays the same.

Why?
Water in its liquid state takes up less space than when it is solid. So, when the ice melts, the water does not spill over the rim of the glass.

Ice floats

The expansion (spreading out or enlargement) of water into the solid state means that ice is less dense than water, and so ice floats. In nature, this characteristic of water is very important. When ice floats on the surface of the seas at the North and South Poles, it makes a protective barrier so that many living things can survive the freezing cold until the ice thaws and the weather becomes less harsh.

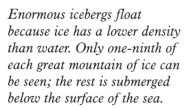

Enormous icebergs float because ice has a lower density than water. Only one-ninth of each great mountain of ice can be seen; the rest is submerged below the surface of the sea.

When the temperature drops below 0°C (32°F), dew becomes frost.

Clouds are made by drops of water coming together. If clouds come into contact with very cold air, these drops change into ice crystals and join together to form snowflakes.

At 0°C (32°F), water solidifies into ice, which takes up more space than water in its liquid state.

Water solutions

Water makes up 60 percent of our body. Most of the water on our planet is a solution of salt and water; and although rivers and lakes are known as freshwater, they also contain dissolved salts. Spectacular underground caves with their stalactites (hanging down) and stalagmites (rising up) have been formed by countless drops of water rich in calcium carbonate constantly dripping and solidifying.

What happens to a substance when it dissolves in water?

TO DISSOLVE OR NOT TO DISSOLVE?

You need:
- 7 small glasses (not colored)
- water
- teaspoon
- small quantities of salt, sand, sugar, rice, honey, ground coffee, and instant coffee

What to do:
1 Fill all the glasses with water.

2 Put 1 teaspoon of one substance in each glass. Mix carefully with the water.

What happens?
Some substances (sugar, salt, honey, and instant coffee) dissolve in the water, coloring it a little. Others (sand, rice, and ground coffee) stay suspended in the water during the mixing, then sink to the bottom or float in the water.

Why?
If a substance dissolves in water (seeming to disappear into it), the water molecules are able to slide between the molecules of the substance and separate them. The soluble (dissolvable) substance does not settle down in a layer in the water in which it is dissolved (the solvent). But if the molecules of the substance are impervious to (can withstand) the water, they remain intact and easily visible. In this case we say that the substance is not soluble in water.

SATURATION LEVEL

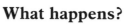

You need:
- two glasses
- teaspoon
- cane sugar
- hot and cold water

What to do:
1 Fill one of the glasses halfway with cold water.

2 Count how many teaspoons of sugar you can dissolve in the water. Stop when sugar remains visible and sinks to the bottom.

3 Fill the second glass halfway with hot water.

4 Count how many teaspoons of sugar you can dissolve in this glass.

What happens?
More sugar can be dissolved in the hot water than in the cold water.

Why?
When no more sugar can be dissolved in water, we say that the solution is saturated. Heat makes water able to dissolve more sugar molecules. The solution that is obtained in this way is called supersaturated. When the supersaturated solution cools down, the excess sugar will be seen at the bottom.

Substances that are soluble in water dissolve in it.

Do soluble substances evaporate with the water?

SALT CRYSTALS

You need:

- table salt
- two glasses
- length of thread
- small plate
- spoon
- water

What to do:

1 Pour cold water into the two glasses.

2 Put salt in both glasses, mixing it until you can add no more.

3 Link the two glasses with a thread, so that the two ends dip well into the water. Put the plate under the part of the thread that hangs down between the two glasses.

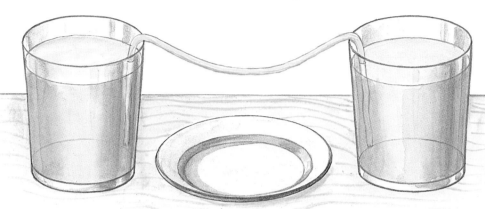

Salt in the home

The salt we use with our food is mostly extracted from salty seas. Big, shallow tanks are built in coastal regions and these fill up with seawater. The heat from the Sun makes the water evaporate, leaving the salt that forms crystals on the bottom of the tanks. If we wanted to obtain pure water from the sea, we would have to reclaim the evaporated water by cooling it down to make it condense. The process by which the solvent (salt) is separated from the solution (seawater) is called distillation.

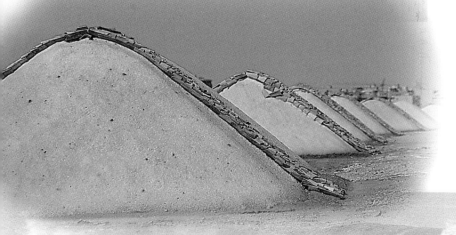

What happens?

After a day or so, salt crystals form on the thread and on the plate.

Why?

The saltwater moves through the thread by capillary action. The water evaporates from the thread (and from the plate, where some droplets fall), leaving the salt, which solidifies into crystals. (The molecules join together to form a geometric pattern.)

Salty and not so salty

Not all seas contain the same amount of salt. The saltiest seas are those where the rate of evaporation is high and there is very little flowing water or rainwater – such as the Red Sea. Seas that are less salty are those where the rate of evaporation is low and water constantly flows into them – for example, the Baltic Sea.

A very salty sea

The Dead Sea is not a sea, but a lake! It contains about 280g (10 oz.) of salt for each liter (quart) of water. The Dead Sea is so salty because it is situated in a place with a very hot and dry climate and also because it does not have a river outlet. Therefore water escapes only by evaporation, causing a strong solution of salt in the water that remains. And since saltwater is more dense than freshwater, anyone can easily float in the Dead Sea, even without swimming!

On the banks of the Dead Sea, evaporation creates spectacular salt structures.

SEPARATE A SOLUTION

You need:
- instant coffee
- saucepan
- two spoons
- water
- match

What to do:

1 Ask an adult to boil water in the saucepan. Carefully pour the water into the cup and dissolve a spoonful of coffee in it.

2 Hold a cold, dry spoon in the steam that rises up from the cup.

What happens?
After a few moments, drops of water form on the spoon. Wait until the drops cool, then taste them. They will be pure water, not coffee.

Why?
Heat makes the water evaporate, but not the coffee. When the steam comes into contact with the cold surface of the spoon, it condenses into drops of pure water. You can do the same test with water and salt. The drops that condense will always be pure water.

Evaporation separates water solutions.
Only the pure water evaporates.

Designing better ships

Specially built basins or canals are used to carry out experiments on miniature models of ships that have been designed but not yet built. For example, the shape of the prow (the front part of the ship) may be adapted for the best penetration of the water. These tanks are very large. They can be up to 900 meters (3,000 ft.) long, up to 24 meters (80 ft.) wide, and up to 6 meters (20 ft.) deep. The models of ships can be up to 9 meters (30 ft.) long, and are equipped with various systems to test how they move through the water. The resistance of water on the movement of the ship is measured with a large dynamometer (which measures the force of the thrust) connected to the model with a cable, or by an electrical instrument. The results of these measurements can be used to change or improve the design of the ship when it is being built.

Fish stay afloat

How do fish swim at different depths? Most fish have a swim bladder, a sac situated behind the stomach, which contains oxygen, nitrogen, and carbon dioxide. By increasing or decreasing the volume of this bladder and therefore its content of gases, fish can change their density and so move up or down in the water.

Water in the human body

60–70 percent of the human body is water. But which parts of the body have the greatest percentage of water? The most "watery" part is the vitreous membrane in the eye, which is 99.68 percent water. The parts with the least amount of water are the teeth and the skeleton, which contain only 2 percent water.

Flotation

In some countries, such as Sweden and Finland, the natural movement of water is used as a means of transportation. Enormous numbers of tree trunks cut down in the forests can be carried along by the current of the rivers. The logs are transported downriver, where they are gathered together by special barriers.

Rivers, seas, lakes

The longest river in the world: the Nile, 6,670 km (4,140 mi.) long

The deepest sea: the Pacific Ocean, which in the Mariana Trench reaches a depth of 11,022 meters (36,161 ft.)

The largest lake: the Caspian Sea, 371,000 km^2 (143,000 sq. mi.) in area

The highest waterfall in the world: Angel Falls in Venezuela, which falls from a height of 972 meters (3,190 ft.)!

Salter Ducks

The energy of ocean waves can be used to produce electricity, although not in very large quantities. The device used for this purpose is called the Salter Duck, because it is shaped much like a toy duck and is named after its English inventor, Professor Stephen Salter. The "duck" is positioned on the surface of the sea in such a way that it is hit on its point by the waves, which move the "beak" back and forth. This action powers a pump that is connected to an electricity generator.

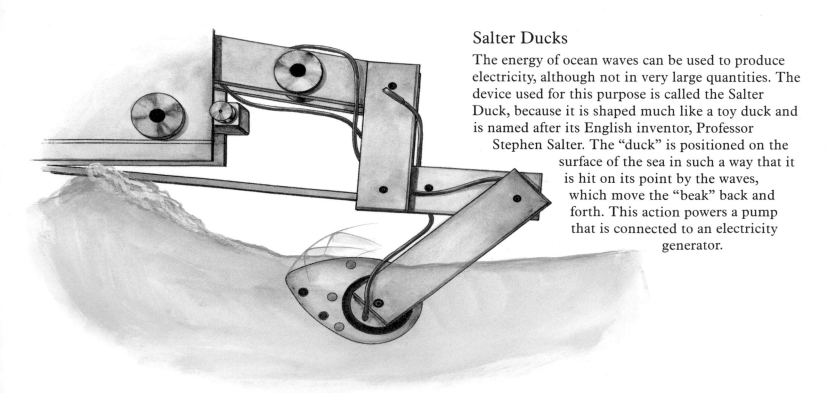

Metric Conversion Table

When you know:	Multiply by:	To find:
inches (in.)	2.54	centimeters (cm)
feet (ft.)	0.3048	meters (m)
yards (yd.)	0.9144	meters (m)
miles (mi.)	1.609	kilometers (km^2)
square feet (sq. ft.)	0.093	square meters (m^2)
square miles (sq. mi.)	2.59	square kilometers (km^2)
acres	0.405	hectares (ha)
quarts (qt.)	0.946	liters (l)
gallons (gal.)	3.785	liters (l)
ounces (oz.)	28.35	grams (g)
pounds (lb.)	0.454	kilograms (kg)
tons	0.907	metric tons (t)

To convert degrees Fahrenheit (°F) to degrees Celsius (°C), subtract 32, then multiply by $\frac{5}{9}$.

Glossary

Archimedes' Principle: scientific law that states that an object totally or partially submerged in a liquid displaces a volume of liquid that weighs the same as the object

bathyscaphe: an underwater vessel used for exploration and research deep in the ocean

capillary action: the force that makes liquids move into or out of tiny passageways such as narrow tubes or small holes in solid materials

concave: curving inward

concentric: sharing the same center point

condensation: the act of changing from a gas to a liquid

convection: the circulation of molecules through a liquid or gas. Warmer liquid or gas rises, and cooler liquid or gas descends.

current: a moving mass of seawater

density: how heavy or light an object or substance is for its size. Density is determined by dividing an object's mass by its volume.

displace: to push something else away. A floating object displaces some of the liquid it floats on.

distillation: the process of purifying a liquid by heating it until it turns into a gas and then letting the gas cool to form a liquid again

dynamometer: an instrument used to measure force

evaporation: the change of a substance from a liquid to a gas

geyser: a hole in the ground through which hot water and steam shoot up in bursts

gravity: the naturally occuring force that attracts objects toward the center of Earth

humidity: the amount of water vapor present in the atmosphere

hydroelectric plant: a factory that produces electricity from water power

insulate: to cover with a material that does not let heat pass through

molecule: the smallest part of a substance that has all the properties of the substance. A molecule is made up of one or more atoms.

soluble: able to be dissolved in a liquid

solution: a mixture made by dissolving a substance in a liquid

solvent: a liquid in which other substances dissolve

surface tension: the force that holds the molecules on the surface of a liquid together in a thin, elastic skin

vapor: a substance in its gaseous state

For Further Reading

Asimov, Isaac. *Asimov's Chronology of Science and Discovery.* New York: HarperCollins, 1994.

Flanagan, Alice K. *Water.* Minneapolis: Compass Point Books, 2000.

Fleisher, Paul. *Liquids and Gases.* Minneapolis: Lerner Publications Company, 2002.

————. *Matter and Energy.* Minneapolis: Lerner Publications Company, 2002.

Kahl, Jonathan D. *Weatherwise.* Minneapolis: Lerner Publications Company, 1996.

Kerrod, Robin. *Planet Earth.* Minneapolis: Lerner Publications Company, 2000.

Walker, Sally M. *Water Up, Water Down: The Hydrologic Cycle.* Minneapolis: Carolrhoda Books, Inc., 1992.

Wick, Walter. *A Drop of Water: A Book of Science and Wonder.* New York: Scholastic Books, 1997.

Wood, Robert W. *Who?: Famous Experiments for the Young Scientist.* Philadelphia: Chelsea House Publishers, 1999.

Websites

Cool Science, sponsored by the U.S. Department of Energy
<http://www.fetc.doe.gov/coolscience/index.html>

The Franklin Institute Science Museum online
<http://www.fi.edu/tfi/welcome.html>

NPR's *Sounds Like Science* site
<http://www.npr.org/programs/science>

PBS's *A Science Odyssey* site
<http://www.pbs.org/wgbh/aso>

Science Learning Network
<http://www.sln.org>

Science Museum of Minnesota
<http://www.smm.org>

Index

Archimedes' Principle, 19

bathyscaphe, 8

capillary action, 7, 32
condensation, 26, 27, 33
convection, 10, 11

density, 10, 21, 22, 23, 29, 33
displacement, 19–21
distillation, 32, 33

evaporation, 24, 26, 32, 33

geysers, 25

hydroelectric energy, 9, 34

molecules, 10, 12, 14, 15, 28, 32

Salter Ducks, 34
sea currents, 11
soap bubbles, 16–17
steam energy, 25
surface tension, 12–17

vapor, 24, 26, 27

water: and energy generation, 6, 9, 25, 34; and
    floating, 18–23; force of, 6–9; and the human
    body, 30, 34; movement of, 6–11; precipitation,
    24, 26, 27, 29; in solutions, 30–33; surface
    tension of, 12–17; transformation of, 24–29;
    water vapor, 24, 26, 27

Photo Acknowledgments

The photographs in this book are reproduced by permission of: Sioen, G., 5, 6, 52–53; Picard, 8; Rives, C., 11; Ledoux, T., 18; Donati, A., 24–25a; Cirani, N., 25b; Veggi, G., 27a, 32; Romano, L., 27b; Staquet, D., 28–29a; Bertaggia, E., 29b; Revy, J.C., 29c; De Gregorio, A., 30; Vergani, A., 33. Front cover (top): South African Tourist Board; front cover (bottom): Corbis Royalty Free Images; back cover (bottom): © Jeff Greenberg

Illustrations by Pier Giorgio Citterio.

About the Author

Antonella Meiani is an elementary schoolteacher in Milan, Italy. She has written several books and has worked as a consultant for many publishing houses. With this series, she hopes to offer readers the opportunity to have fun with science, to satisfy their curiosity, and to learn essential concepts through the simple joy of experimentation.